encapsulated emotions

encapsulated emotions

by rha arayal

Copyright © RHA ARAYAL 2020

Supervising Editors: L. Austen Johnson, Emily Oliver

Associate Editor(s): Rebecca Hane, Shannon Marks

Internal Formatting: Alexandria Boykin

Interior Illustrator: Tirion Lewis

Cover Designer: Tirion Lewis

ISBN (Print): 978-1-952919-40-4

ISBN (eBook): 978-1-952919-41-1

GenZPublishing.org

Aberdeen, NJ

the life cycle of a time capsule follows the evolution of our emotions:

collection, preservation, and decay.

like most things in life, emotions are temporary.

therefore, we must encapsulate and treasure them until they perish.

contents

PART ONE — collection   1

PART TWO — preservation   33

PART THREE — decay   63

PART ONE

collection

rha arayal

atlas

he had the greatest burden;
he held the sins of a population.
he balanced tragedies and heartbreaks
until his blood became the icy lakes.

the rain made it heavy
like condensation on a windscreen.
he sputtered like an old Chevy,
but he wasn't a machine.

he staggered and cried.
then he took deep breaths
and tried,
harder,

until his fists were
a part of bustling Tokyo
and barren Sahara.

he longed for a wife—
he'd cherish her like a pearl.
he'd had a lonely life, so
he'd give her the world

and escape—
but you can't
shift the weight
of fate.

meanwhile
we built towers
and flower gardens;
they pierced his eyes
and blurred his vision.

humanity has uncanny precision
when it comes to deathly decisions.

he folded neatly,
vibrations like shivers.
his veins crossed like roads,
and his blood flowed like rivers.

his blue eyes became the seas,
his skin the caramel coffee beans.
his body became a feast
to map out—

i hope that his soul has found peace

and not a blackout;
he blew like a fuse
and lived a futile life,
but his story comes to use
on a long car drive.

i imagine that he
sits on a cloud and
conducts the rain.

i imagine that he's
found an antidote
for pressurised stains.

i imagine that he
sits on a cloud and
conducts our pain.

the strawberry field that we call women

only here for your nourishment,
we're expected to cut off
the rotten parts of us.

you want our souls served
on a china plate.
you don't care until
it's too late,
until we're
fading away.

but we are
more beautiful
than fruit,
surviving all seasons,
blossoming
through the night.

wasted pages

i could change the world.
it would be as easy as
dotting an i.
i watch you sigh—
but listen.

humans are plights.
i'll give you my wings
so that you can take flight

this is aggravating though—
i am saying
that i'd burn my pages,
spill my ink,
pour my words,
and cease to think.

i'd cut off my tongue
to give you a taste;
i'd tie my own hands
and never escape.

fairy tales

you'd think that fairy tales
would be fairly benign—
but they're filled with
treacherous signs
and hierarchy lines.

"mummy!
one more chapter,
one more page."

why would i read a story
where a girl has no say?

she sits in the tower and waits.
she kisses a prince and faints.
she has a happy-ever-after fate.

why would i read a story
full of patriarchal drawl
and superficial scrawls?

he slays the dragon.
he saves the day.

he holds her in his arms
and murmurs, "it's okay."

he doesn't get sweaty palms,
she doesn't reapply lip balm.

love songs are sung,
battles are won,
but do we want this to be
the future of our young?

the garden in my mind

a sanctuary for sonnets.
pollenated ideas,
buzzing thoughts,

the Garden of Eden
couldn't be more—

more alive,
more guarded
at the gates;

for each dawning day,
we await ambush—

for sinners
to rush in,
pluck ripe apples
from our trees,

and then leave.

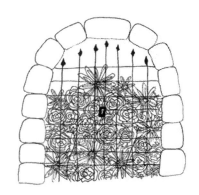

the wind sings to me

the leaves rustle in the breeze.
the branches interlock,
or so it seems.

each creek is
in harmony.

what i seek,
i cannot see—

the wind sings to me
and guides me home;
the leaves flutter like eyelashes
and remind me i'm not alone.

the wind does not segregate;
you will hear a reedy voice,
if you listen and wait.

the colours of freedom

the soft-hued colours mix
like moths and butterflies.

the pale colours fit
like bread, cheese, and wine.

the pastel colours swirl
like confidence and white lies.

the vivid colours drip
like a cold-air sunrise.

the glowing colours lift
like feathers that intertwine.

the sun and the sea

make me feel free.

the shades of space

stardust settles

like sand

on my skin.

a kaleidoscope

of colours,

vivid but thin.

i wonder what

gaining sight brings.

i wonder why

we question everything

when the answers

patiently lay

beneath our feet—

when the answers

make homes

between our teeth.

letter to my student self

you perfectionist.
you beautiful wreck.
you scrambling mess.

let me tell you now
that your best
isn't all-nighters.

your best isn't stressed.

i know it feels unavoidable;
even when your desk is clear,
revision cards clutter your mind,

but it's time
to be kind
to yourself—

you're only human.

the feelings that we hide

they follow us like shadows
during the day.

they reside in our throats
in the words we'll never say.

they tickle our tongues
and laugh as we choke,
teasing us to vocalise
the feelings that we cloak—
the feelings that we hide.

they prod us to
memorise this
bittersweet pride.

as they shriek, we sigh.
we lie in rows,
our bodies close,
but never intertwined.

we lie on dewy grass
and stare at the skies.

we live in bubbles
and relish this life.

we run away from
our troubles,
but our mistakes
turn us to rubble
in ways that
aren't subtle.

panic attacks
when we realise
that we lack
in empathy.

we look to
the storm
and cry,

"no

seasonal sadness

a casual madness
that seeps into
your home,
the type of cold
that splits your bones.

although happiness
is romanticised,
truth be told,
it is unattainable—
like a sun of gold.

the exposed trees
may look unsteady
but, like you,
they are ready to say
goodbye to the past—
ready to be brand new.

seasonal sadness
isn't a lifetime of madness;
the casual cold is,
truth be told,

the realest thing

you'll ever know.

treasure untouched

fake smiles work for a while,
and then they get tiring.

i ask you to stop admiring
the character i play
and the excuses i make.

each compliment is fake,
each bitter remark real.

in my brain,
there's a chest and it's sealed.

it keeps me sane, being locked away,
but the paint has started to peel.

it numbs the pain,
but today i started to feel.

you are home

my brain and heart
reject this body.
it is not enough
to sustain
rash decisions
and insecurities.

my nerves,
poisoned by
the anxiety
in my veins;

my bloodstream,
contaminated by
this mess,
this mind,
is breaking at
the seams.

even if the
world ends,
you are my home.
even if the

universe implodes,

you are the sun

shining through.

for years

the atmosphere

was blue.

for years

i was

homeless,

searching

every avenue.

that was, until

i met you.

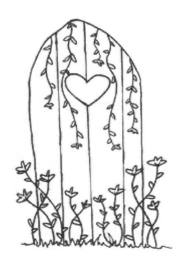

sorrow society

shaking hands
can unite;
sullen eyes
can see the light;
broken souls
can write.

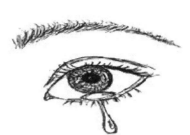

if i lead the way,
we can all
catch sight
of something bigger
than us,
more complicated
than love,
more inspiring
than the skies above;

we can all
become members
of a sorrow society.

but i only want you

there are more fish in the sea;
the whole concept
drowns me.

salty water pours into
my wounds—
the ones that you formed.

on those nights,
when the tidal storm of
thoughts keeps me up,
i tiptoe to my window
and i gaze up
at the sky.

a million stars,
but i only want you.

the price

the demons that i fight
sometimes look like the light,
so i give darkness a try;
if i'm found out, i have to lie,

but self-destruction is sometimes
an attractive find . . .

people are taught to be kind,
but lessons never cover
talking to depressed types.

having a lover is nice
until they bother you—

but there's
a price
for every view.

my body, a tapestry

my cross-stitched eyebrows furrow,
shimmering with sequins.

pearls jut out my spine
like the beads of a necklace.

behind me, i cover the bland—
this whitewashed wall
has drowned out many faces.

my body, a tapestry,
contains more stories
than the Bible holds.

my heart is colder
than winter rain.
my eyes glint with
overflowing pain.

my body, a tapestry,
a visual that screams
"i'm not sane."

insomniac for you

phone notification—
my world is
alight.

a glaring blue screen
all through
the night.

daylight restricts
the time of
our digital lives.

all i want to do
is be
an insomniac for you.

two coffee-drowned
minds,
two people that
think alike.

two sleep cycles,
cracked,
like our iPhone screens—
two insomniacs.

matchbox men

they set the world alight
with their power-hungry ways.

they exist to start fights;
their ruling is just a phase.

they exist to fill
a fact-box history page.

they exist to kill
and mic-drop centre stage.

raised by their ideals
and lack of morals,

nurtured by bloodshed
and their parent's quarrels—

matchbox men.

they rise like flames.

the earth is just a teenage girl

she screams
"you used me!
you abused me!"
like a teenage girl
to her first love.

but she's not just
any teenage girl.

she grew each
sapling into a tree;
she's witnessed
the making of every sea.

every day
she breaks.
we owe her
much for
her strength—

just like
any other
teenage girl.

a feminist's fear

i fear the day
when i will have
limited words
to say.

i will step out
into the world,
the floor cluttered
with poached
birds.

society will have won,
a world run by your
sons.

we smile,
attempt
to seem free,
until the wrinkles
in our skin
replicate
the dead
trees.

we smile,

attempt

to seem free,

and from those

same mouths,

we cannot

speak.

i fear the day when

the little girls can

no longer play.

i fear the day when

the men take

everything away.

rha arayal

PART TWO

preservation

rha arayal

some homes

some homes
have love etched into the walls,
underneath each aging
crayon scribble.

some homes
are cluttered with memories,
even when the toy box is put away
and the rugs are cleaned.

some homes
are empty
without their people.

some homes
are collective bodies
of our happy place,
of our love source.

some homes
are called

sanctuaries.

(i confide in search engines)

i am defined by my pursuit of answers.

"why do my hands shake
(when i overthink)?"

"how to bake
(without burnt cookies in the sink)?"

"am i depressed?
(i cry too much—is it stress)?"

"how to impress someone
(anyone)?"

"how to make friends
(laugh at my puns)?"

most times
asking questions helps,

but, sometimes,
i want to delve
inside of my brain.

i'd set the weather so
it never rained.

i'd turn off the circling question marks.
i'd erase all the stretch marks.
maybe then people could look for
answers in me—

but until then,
Google knows me

better than my friends do.

your white privilege

i don't think
it's a nice phrase.
it's used by us,
the POC as you say,
to call out your foul play,
very much to your
petty dismay.

we don't even
ask for you to pay—
just to listen to what
we have to say.

you use the hashtag,
upload the black snap,
that you don't understand.

don't say to me
"well, you're not black"
because,
well,
i'm not white either.

you have called me
an "exotic" creature,
rubbing your hands
together like a
zookeeper.

you have made us
the underachievers.
you snicker and say
"we're employing cleaners."

beneath the weight
of the "economy,"
i too have said
"i can't breathe."

your glossed over eyes
and crumpled face
look like perfect origami,
brimming with grace.

if you can overlook
George's story
without being shook—
if you can say
"black lives matter"

without a falter—

from the pain

that remains

in those three words,

then *your* white privilege

goddamn shows.

we're almost the same

"rest assured,
we're broken too!"

celebrities
claim their
lives are bitter
behind closed
doors.

they post
flawless pictures
just to make
you insecure.

they advertise
anti-blemish products
and teeth whitening kits
to their audience
of kids—

they preach
"you are the future!"
to little girls.

the next day

they teach

"how to get a suitor,"

as if our goals

are their goals,

as if our lives

are defined

by voting on

their polls,

by adding to

their payroll.

news presenters

could be plastic—

manicured hands

and shiny smiles.

voices buzz

through the radio,

voices travel

miles and miles.

only occasionally

do they cough

or stutter—

it jolts you,

like a car engine

sputter.

wait...

you, too, have a family,

a home,

and not a

warehouse of clones?

wait...

have i fallen

for the bait?

is my mind warped?

am i too late

to realise that

we're almost

the same?

you, too, have blood

in your veins—

plaster a smile

on your face.

you, too, wake up,

pretending that

everything's okay.

magician's assistant

you saw *us* in half
yet we receive applause second.

you make us disappear,
but we're more *here*
than you reckoned.

you banish us from stage,
you lock us in a cage,

yet we escape—
yet we remain…
unscathed.

magic is not an illusion.
it is perfumed fusion
of a magician's assistant—

her steady high-heeled stride
and the fact that you *want* her to die.

she flashes her white teeth
like clean piano keys;

the audience swoons.

she waves her dazzling hands
and lies alone
in her coffin of doom.

superficial distractions

they're everywhere.
when social interaction drains us,
we use double taps to
recharge our souls.

but how many more posts
until we fade, like ghosts?
when ten likes take half a day,
we laugh and say, "it's okay."

yet we're not full inside—
too many comparisons
yet to be made,
and when our friends
don't comment
we feel so betrayed.

they are everywhere.
religion
to restore faith,
to validate,
to pray,
who would be gay

when you can wish your
worries away?
and by that i mean
nothing cruel or mean,
just that this new life has brought
more than we've yet been taught.

it seems
people would rather
live through a filter
than just be themselves—
be a little unfamiliar.

they are everywhere.
intoxicate your mind
whatever will earn you
the label:
that kid who's so unstable
 —the addict
to superficial distractions.

polluted bloodstream

tears that run without me,
demons that exist to spite me,
thoughts that swirl to doubt me,
moods that leave me pouting…

i sniffle, i sigh
i slam doors, i cry

the cycle repeats
as hard as i try.

hopes and dreams
aren't what they seem.
no one wants me;
i have a polluted bloodstream.

my eyes drift like daydreams,
my soul diluted, yet it gleams
with sorrow and with jealousy—

i hope tomorrow
i can take each fatality,
each tragedy, i'll borrow
and capture in an arrow

to pierce my bone marrow.

drugged

society's fumes make
factories look pure.

glance at what you want to see,
listen to who you want to be,
take pills to calm your mind,
conform to rot what's inside.

whose am i?
do i belong to wet concrete
and bulletin board lights?

just a kid; i'm also sick.
too much screen for my eyes,
too much listening to these lies.

whose am i?
i'm bored of these games.
i'm bored of grabbing at rope
for it to give way.

so pull the plug, cut the cord,
listen to me!
you are yours.

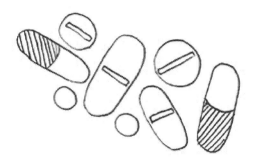

acquired taste

my stomach might not be flat.
the workouts
haven't worked out yet;
they still owe me a
six pack.

my digestive system
works just fine,
but it prefers food
that i could never dine.

it consumes
hurt and betrayal;
without my daily dose
i would look pale.

for breakfast,
it eats insanity,
not toast.

what can i say...
i have the most
acquired taste.

humans/the devil

the world without humans
is like Hell without the devil.

it would be fun
if we were mere skeletons—
vegetation would thrive
and each manufactured beehive
would swarm with life.

don't believe the lies
that crackle between wires.
they're fed to us
through hospital tubes.
if humans left,
the devil would too.

in reality,
we are a fatality—
a slow-spreading poison
that leads to insanity.

if this place we call home
was cluttered with our bones,

we wouldn't even deserve gravestones.

us humans

do nothing but meddle—

if we died,

so would the devil.

inner development

i'm tired of
making up
excuses for you
in my mind
for why you
couldn't find time.

i'm tired of
excusing
the hastiness
in your air
and the
harsh gravity
that you bare.

at a later date,
a better time,
with some
kinder friends,
and finer wine,

we'll laugh about it
and it'll be too late

for you to come back.

book of lies

you wrote the story wrong,
calling survivors
victims,
calling trauma
disease.

so i ripped the
patriarchal pages out.

we're not vulnerable,
we're fighters.

next time you
write a book,
write about something

you actually care about.

ink blood

a tattoo across my heart,
a logo inside my arteries.

a rush in my veins,
droplets that expand.

colours that collide,
substance that stains—
ink.

crimson that crawls,
stains that stay—
blood.

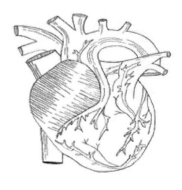

melancholy moon, do you cry too?

beneath his glowing presence
is a failing skeleton.

under his ominous stare
is a lifeless soul.

his crescent shadow
reminds him that
he's not whole.

a boy
whose eyes
are battered
and barren—

he, too,
tosses
and turns.

he, too,
holds the
capability
to feel blue.

a boy

watches the

melancholy moon,

his masculinity

strung out

towards the stars.

he says,

"do you cry too?"

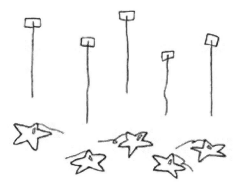

change is coming.

i promise
the worst
always gets better,
no matter how bad you feel.
don't write your goodbye letter,

even if trying
is a little bit tiring.
i'll be the caffeine
on your Monday mornings;
please stay awake.

i feel it.
one more day,
a happy pill
to make it more okay,

change is coming.
you deserve a new start.
don't let this break you.
just hang on…
change is coming.

broken glass city

we soared through ceilings,
but only if our exteriors
were appealing.

we swung from chandeliers
until they felt gnawing fear,
until they called us down
by whispering, "dear…"

we scratched stereotypes
until they no longer moulded
to body types.

the glass shards pierce
and our wounds run red.
some words are better
shouted than said.

we pulled skyscrapers down.
there are no housewives around town,
there are no hushing-the-baby sounds,

because we are fierce and loud.
we aren't your 'dear's,
we are proud.

PART THREE

decay

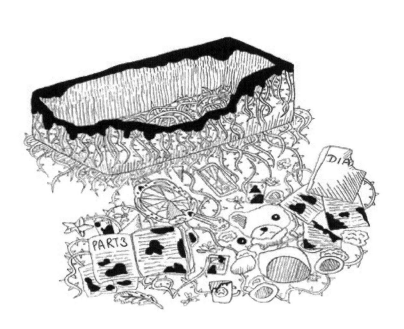

rha arayal

never alone

these bones—
cold.
this home—
empty,
or so i'm told.

shadows dance
when the radio plays.
memories come alive
when i hear your name.

the ghost of you remains.

goodbye, grandmother

i clutched her crumpled hands
and shook my head.

my tongue stumbled
through a goodbye
in a language that's faded,
like newsprint in the sun.

when will i return
to this country?
to my home?

Grandmother,
i honestly don't
know your first name.

you know me as
"the London one,"
the one who's "not the same."

i stand out of this tradition
like a mirror that won't reflect.

this relationship is complex—
my words are a stutter
and your days are numbered.

i want to ask, i want to say:
have you ever been
out of the country?
have you ever been
on a train?

i bet you imagine us flying away,
every time with heavy eyes…

but this is the price we pay.

sorry mum/you were right

i hate watching
my mother cry.

i hate watching
the woman
who guided me
lose herself.

i hate watching
my origin
of nurture
feel so alone.

more often than not,
we are the source of
their pain.
we are the poison in
their veins.

after every
"sorry mum"
the guilt remains.

after every
"you were right,"
we tell ourselves
we'll never fight
again.

it is you
i depend on,
that helped me
clutch my first crayon;

it is you
that held me,

yet you never
prepared me
for feeling
this way.

i want to say
"i'm sorry,
you were right."

in hindsight,
you were
my sunlight.

you grew me from
seed to sapling.
you smiled through
collapsing.

my teen years
were a fool's.
i didn't see the sacrifice.

when i have
my own children,
i'll see that you
were no villain.

when i have
my own children
i'll wish
i'd listened.

ocean of forgotten names

diary pages,
folded like boats.

empty lungs,
the corpses float.

water seeps through
a waterproof coat.

in a glass bottle,
a single note:

"i can't breathe."

they never could.

the death was slow,
air like poison.

why were they chosen
to die by corrosion -

the deterioration of

our equality notions?

why was it them
that died out in the open,
alone and deserted,
scarred and broken?

why did God give
them life if

the world is frozen?

falling (out of love)

sheets to my chin,
cold air grips my skin.

heart throbbing,
i need you now
more than ever

you, my accomplishment.
my sweet endeavour—

but out you slip
through my fingertips...

there are parts of you i won't miss,
parts i could easily list.

i embrace the frost
as it settles on my skin

our love is lost.
perhaps i won't miss it…

me, the manic mumbler.

me, falling

into a deep slumber.

purpose?

my purpose
has been stripped of me.
my train of thought
has been derailed.

my steady port has sailed
into welcoming waves;

my skeleton is the shadow
that cowers in the caves;

dodging the
jutting edges,

humming
patriotic pledges,

this is a country
of ruin—
what are we doing?

trimming
green hedges.

buying
snow sledges.

that is my country
you're accusing—

what are you doing?

smashed mirror

a reflection of my soul,
which craves to be whole.

i recollect my thoughts.
i gather the pieces.

the edges pierce,
burning fragile skin.

my veins churn.

there she comes,
drop by drop.
there she comes
from destructive deeds.

i bleed.

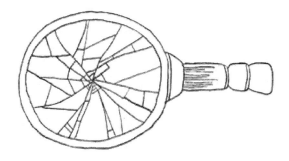

i forget so many things

i forget that i have
searched faces
for memories and love.

i forget that i have
held their gazes
and felt
no recollection…

i've found their freckles
to be a misleading map,
a collapsed constellation.

i've found their insipid pupils
untraceable
to time or place.

i forget that i have
seen strangers—
other realms
of humanity—
on the streets.

i forget that i have

seen strangers

with stories foreign

to the page into my skin.

champagne rain

mould has flowered on the windowpanes.
the concrete cracks are no longer plain.

they contain
blossoming stains
of human neglect.

they contain
the numbing pain
of nature in effect.

rain has showered like champagne.
the occurrence of the mundane
has been brutally slain—

nature has erased
all that was humane;

nature has rewritten
the plot of this play.

she has cut the puppet strings,
chastised us with bee stings.

she orchestrates the music

of our violins.

she controls the consequences

of our sins.

judgement day

has the world made its mark
on you, once a simple soul?
are you shattered or whole?

has the sun
etched freckles
on your face?
have your feet
walked you to
your favourite place?
has your busy mind
gone insane?

have your cheeks
bloomed red
from the humid air?
have your calves
ached from
those steep stairs?

you've lived
a lifetime,
you lived it well,

but now it's
up to Him...
do you belong
in Heaven
or in Hell?

has your skin
started to fold?
has your brain
started to mould
to society's norms?

off you go
to your
eternal holiday.
as much as you try,
you can't keep
death at bay...
but are you small enough
to fit into the suitcase?

off you go.
say goodbye
with grace.

you've lived

a lifetime,

you lived it well,

but now it's

up to Him...

do you belong

in Heaven

or in Hell?

the girl/the ghost

although
she is warm
to the touch,
and her eyes
light up,

there are only
teeth in her smile.

she's nothing
but a being;
she's incapable
of feeling.

the girl/
the ghost

the body/
the host.

salty tears

when i cry,
many things happen.

salty tears
stain inky pages—
they fuse
flimsy white
with deep blue.

my head hurts.
like a betrayed lover,
or a lone orca,

i crave comfort,
pulling spears from
my chest
and swimming
in circles.

but much to
my dismay,
my pain
can't be erased.

my wounds
won't heal,
ever.
i'll be alone,
forever.

so these
salty tears,

they act as an
antidote—
an expression.

these salty tears
comfort me.

they lessen
the churning sea
within.

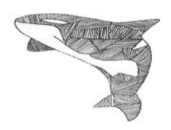

cold world, warm heart

i can't expect

love to grow

on the walls of a home

that's shuddering

from the cold,

that's less bricks

and more mould,

that's on the market

to be sold—

a home

too temporary

and weak,

a home where

the roof leaks,

windows creak,

and the door

is closed.

no one can

love me

when i

should be

more

functional and friendly.

i shouldn't

rely on solitude to defend.

i shouldn't

rely on injustice to mend.

so i'll close the

rotting windows gently—

they are incapable

of protecting me

from the storm

of "I SHOULD BE MORE!"

the home that i need

is inside me—

i have a heart that's warm.

song to society

oh, your love is costly—

tears for likes,
screams for fights.

society, you ruin me.
ban animal cruelty!
society, you're like jewellery
that's been sourced brutally.

trends get reinforced
by daytime TV,
by catwalks,
by festivals under marquees.

society, you ruin me.
ban human cruelty!
society, i beg you
for translucency,
not ambiguity.

stop your phoney guarantees.
stop your waves of anxiety.

stop losing the keys

to my real identity.

oh, your love costs me.

dear humanity

i love you,
but you are
the worst thing
in this world.

dear humanity,
i sometimes forget
that i am a part of you.

dear humanity,
i am ashamed to
be a part of you,

and contribute
to the pain,
to the global waste,
to the making of chains,
to the polluted aftertaste
of our presence.

dear humanity,
this is just a sentence.
don't cry—
i hate you.

you are why
the sky isn't blue,
the climate is askew,
the sea is cluttered,
the engines sputter.

you are why
i can see this view.
we went to the moon,
i sing my favourite tune,
and new fruits grew.

dear humanity,
we like to consult
and console.
we like to resolve
each heart and soul.

dear humanity,
we like to destroy
and decay.
we like to burn
our home to charcoal.
we like to learn

from our lack of control.

glitter—

it's not something
i can control.

but, if i could,
i'd replace
this rain
with
glitter—
it might make me
more sane and less bitter.

let it
sink in:
into my bloodstream,
into my mind…

let the glitter
take away what isn't mine.

worries and anxieties,
once dull and slight,
to transform into something
pacifying and bright.

all inside of my

minuscule yet

monocular mind.

a paper-thin concept

if people were pieces of paper,
all manufactured,
all the same,

we would be waiting for an artist
to take away our empty pain.

some may become classics
but many would be hollow like plastic;

silver sketches, which could've been more,
paper white intentions—
they clutter the floor.

what about the stacks of paper
at the back of the shelf—

don't they deserve a chance
like everybody else?

i met God in Hell

He was immune
to Satan's lure.

He strolled past sinners,
just to feel pure.

He became
the winner, the creator,
by saving His pride
for later.

but now,
His hair greys
and He spends His days

wishing He had pride
to put aside;

i met God in Hell,
and He only had

bitterness to tell.

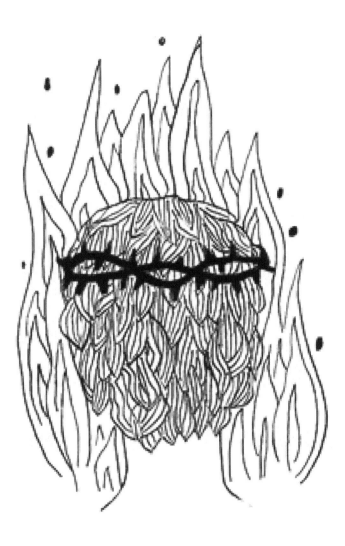

to my best friend

i want to embrace
and erase the days
between us.

head to our
favourite place,
instead of
blank stares
and video games.

i know you're
not dead,
but i'm mourning.

i'm guilty about
each fight—
in hindsight,

i should've been
grateful for you.

no one misses you
like i do.

Thank you for reading

encapsulated emotions

Please consider posting a rating or review. Reviews not only help other readers find books, but they also let readers know which books may end up their new favorite!

ABOUT THE AUTHOR

RHA ARAYAL is a 17-year-old British-Nepalese writer. She loves writing poetry and is inspired by the likes of classical poets such as Emily Dickinson. She aims to raise awareness and project marginalised voices through her writing.

Instagram: @encapsulated_emotions

Find out more on encapsulatedemotions.carrd.co.

ABOUT THE PUBLISHER

GENZ PUBLISHING is on a mission to bring new authors to the world.

It can be nearly impossible for writers with promising talent to be recognized in the publishing and digital media industry. There are many unheard voices in the publishing world because of the often costly (for time, energy, and money) requirements for breaking into it.

Since there often seems to be an under-representation of new and innovative voices in the publishing world, we decided it was time for change.

GenZ Publishing emphasizes new, emerging, young and underrepresented authors. We're not a vanity press. Instead, we're a traditional, indie publisher that focuses on mentoring authors through each step of the publishing process and beyond: editing, writing sequels, cover design, marketing, PR, and even getting agented for future works. We love to see our authors succeed both with the books they publish with us and with their other publications. That's why we call it the "GenZ Family."

OTHER GENZ POETRY COLLECTIONS

Burning the Bacon by L. Austen Johnson

Fragmented Roots by Joanne Zarrillo Cherefko

Pink Marigold Rays by Daniel J. Flore III

Sometimes, I have a heart by K.G. Ginley